Original title:
Baking Gingerbread and Christmas Joy

Copyright © 2024 Creative Arts Management OÜ
All rights reserved.

Author: Ethan Prescott
ISBN HARDBACK: 978-9916-90-868-6
ISBN PAPERBACK: 978-9916-90-869-3

Memories Made in Sweet Confection

In the kitchen, flour flies,
Laughter echoes, oh what a surprise!
Ginger men dance, if you believe,
But some might crumble and take their leave.

Rolling pins clash, oh what a sight,
The dog's in the flour—oh what a fright!
Sticky fingers, a chocolate smear,
With every mishap, we shed a cheer.

The Art of Frosting and Festivity

Pipes of icing, swirls and sways,
Nutty toppings in a glorious haze.
The cat steals a cookie, what a scene,
We chase him around, he's quite the fiend!

Sprinkle sprinkles with glee and care,
Who knew this could turn into a dare?
I take a taste, and oh what a mess,
Maybe I should just settle for less.

Tidings of Comfort and Cookies

The oven's warm, our hearts are too,
Tripping over flour, oh who knew?
Cookies giggle as they start to swell,
Do we create or trap a spell?

With each batch, delight's in the air,
Anticipation of the snouts everywhere.
I laugh at the chaos, can't be coy,
Who needs perfect when there's such joy?

A Spice-laden Symphony

Cinnamon whirls in a dance of despair,
Spoons get tossed, but we don't care.
A batch is burned, oh what a shame,
But we'll eat them all just the same!

Ginger men giggle, stand at attention,
My frosting skills deserve a mention.
A dash of humor, a splash of cheer,
In this sweet mess, we hold dear.

Winter Wonderland in Every Slice

The dough's a bit too sticky,
Yet we dance around the bowl,
Flour flies like snowy flakes,
As laughter takes its toll.

With sprinkles like confetti,
And frosting on our nose,
Each cookie tells a story,
Of how this chaos goes.

Our hands a bit like glue,
As we shape with joy and cheer,
A ginger man with candy arms,
Is the star of the frontier.

When the timer dings its song,
We gather round the treats,
In this slice of winter bliss,
There's no room for defeats.

The Secret Recipe of Togetherness

In the kitchen, pots collide,
Mixing bowls can barely hold,
With giggles rising high,
And stories yet untold.

Mom dropped her measuring cup,
Dad's dancing with the cat,
Flour fights and sugar spills,
Tell me, where's the spat?

A pinch of love, a dash of fun,
Stir it with a grin,
A crazy mix of silly thoughts,
Baking's where we begin.

When the treats come out so fine,
We feast and raise a cheer,
The secret's not the recipe,
But the joy and those held dear.

A Whisk of Winter Magic

With every twist and turn, we make,
A whisking whirlwind in the bowl,
Chasing frostings, sprinkles too,
As giggles fill our souls.

A family of frosty friends,
All lined up in a row,
The snickering snowman winks at me,
As if he really knows.

The oven sings a merry tune,
While timers beep and chime,
We gather round the window hot,
And munching takes its time.

At the end with crumbs galore,
We collapse upon our chairs,
With belly laughs and happy hearts,
What magic fills the air!

Festive Flourishes on the Table

The table's dressed in cookie cheer,
With sprigs of green and red,
Our mountain of delights awaits,
From sweet rolls to gingerbread.

With shapes of stars and candy canes,
A feast for every eye,
We add a wink, some sprinkles too,
As laughter soars up high.

Mom slips and yelps, it's all in fun,
Dad hides some on his plate,
We gobble up the fun we make,
In this grand holiday slate.

The final bake, the final cheer,
We sing of joy and glee,
For every bite is mixed with love,
And sweet camaraderie.

The Comfort of Spice and Home

In the kitchen, flour flies,
Ginger men with silly ties!
Sugar smiles and laughter rise,
Oh, what fun when chaos lies!

Marshmallow snowflakes tumble down,
A gummy bear wears a tiny crown.
Rolling pins dance 'round and 'round,
While silly songs and giggles sound!

Sifting spice, the clock ticks fast,
The doughy blob, too big to last.
With sprinkles on, the shot is cast,
In a tasty race, we laugh and blast!

Out of the oven, they come to play,
A sugar rowdy parade today.
With crumbs and jokes, we'll never sway,
In sweet delight, we sing and stay!

Joyful Moments Stirred Together

Whisking clouds of sugar, oh so bright,
We dropped the egg with quite a fright!
A scoop of fun in every bite,
Our silly chef hats fit just right!

The jelly beans dance with glee,
Marzipan boats sail carefree.
Chocolate chips plot mischief, you see,
While icing rivers flow with a spree!

Laughter spills over the countertop,
As we create a gingerbread flop.
But who could stop this sugar lot?
We nibble while the timers pop!

When all is done, we gather near,
With sticky hands and festive cheer.
The mess we made, we hold so dear,
In every bite, it's love, not fear!

Piping Dreams on a Snowy Eve

In the kitchen, flour flies,
Sugar frolics, oh what a surprise!
Ginger hugs the cheeky spice,
As cookies dance, oh so nice!

Rolling pins are racing fast,
While frosting laughs and dreams are cast.
Sprinkles jump from jar to plate,
Yummy chaos, oh it's fate!

Little ones with doughy hands,
Create their own sweet, wondrous plans!
With every bite, a giggle pops,
As crumbs fall down and nobody stops!

Cookies glow with frosting bright,
As we munch in holiday light.
A taste of laughter, a sprinkle of cheer,
Sweets and smiles, we hold dear!

A Celebration of Warmth and Wonder

The oven hums a jolly tune,
While we whisk and giggle in the afternoon.
Here comes grandma with her grin,
Saying, "Let the fun begin!"

Flour whispers sweet little lies,
As we check if our treats can rise.
With every batch, our hopes will soar,
Sweets galore, who could want more?

Choco chips tumble without care,
We'll eat the dough, oh how we dare!
A sprinkle here, a splash of that,
Merriment in every chat!

With laughter spun through every bite,
Our hearts are warm, our faces bright.
In this kitchen, love's recipe,
Brings joy to every memory!

Sweet Spices of the Season

Stirring pots with a goofy grin,
The spice must flow, let the fun begin!
Nutmeg whispers a cheeky joke,
As cinnamon twirls, oh what a hoax!

Rolling out dough with a splash of flair,
We flour our noses like we don't care!
Each cutout shapes a silly face,
In this sweet, jolly, bustling place!

A taste test here, a nibble there,
Sticky fingers everywhere!
Grandpa chuckles, his belly shakes,
As we decorate with goofy mistakes!

When all is done, we take a seat,
With plates piled high, a tasty treat!
We toast to laughter, silly mess,
In this joyful kitchen, we're truly blessed!

Whispers of Warmth and Sugar

When the snow falls soft and slow,
In the kitchen, sweet scents flow.
Ginger stories told with cheer,
As laughter bubbles, winter's here!

Cookies wink from trays of gold,
Sugar shapes that can't be controlled!
With spatulas like mighty wands,
We create magic with our hands!

The puppy sniffs the crumbs we spill,
As we giggle and chase, what a thrill!
Frosting fingers, full of cheer,
Raining sprinkles far and near!

With every batch, our hearts expand,
Λ festive joy, we'll make a stand!
So here's to sweets and a silly song,
In this warm place, we all belong!

Decorating with Joy and Spice

Sprinkle flour like a snowstorm's dance,
Rolling dough beneath the bright light's glance.
Elves with icing, battling for a prize,
Whiskers of frosting, oh what a surprise!

Gumdrops gather on a sugary hill,
Piping bags burst with enthusiasm's thrill.
Cookies giggle, wearing tiny bows,
We sculpt their smiles with tips and shows.

Holiday Hues on Each Cookie

A rainbow of colors on doughy delight,
Sugar rush madness, oh what a sight!
Red, green, and yellow, a vibrant brigade,
Counting calories? Let's call it a trade!

Cookie cutters dancing like stars in a choir,
Ginger spice whispers, setting hearts on fire.
Sprinkles tumble like confetti so wild,
Just one more bite? Oh, how we're beguiled!

Glistening Icing and Cheerful Hearts

Icing gleams like glitter on top of a dream,
Who knew a cookie could make us all scream?
Frosting mishaps leave us rolling in laughter,
A sticky situation, happy ever after!

Chill in the air but warmth in our souls,
Sweet scents of ginger make us all feel whole.
Each sugary bite's a burst of goodwill,
Even the grumpy can't help but feel thrill!

A Tradition Spun in Ginger

Rolling the dough with grandpa's old hat,
Whiskers of flour, and what's that? A cat!
Anthony sneezes, flour flies like snow,
"Cover your mouth!" but he's all aglow.

Creativity sparking, we mold and we shape,
Every cookie's a critter, or maybe aape?
Bake them until they bring joy to the plate,
A crunchy conclusion that's more than just fate!

The Oven's Embrace

In the kitchen, flour flies,
Laughter echoes, oh what a surprise!
Spices dancing, who will win?
Gingerbread men with mischief and grin.

Batter splatters, kids in a race,
Sugar on noses, frosting a trace.
Rolling pins twirl, chips on the floor,
Who knew that fun could start a dough war?

Cookies giggle, they rise and swell,
A cheeky aroma, casting a spell.
Chocolate drops jump into a fight,
Hoping to be the hero tonight.

With icing's delight, we weave our tales,
Sugar-coated giggles, nothing else fails.
In this warm corner, our hearts align,
Each little treat is a moment divine.

Frosted Dreams of December

Whisking up dreams, a swirl and a plop,
As we skip and dance, like tops that won't stop.
Each cookie that bakes holds a giggle inside,
Waiting for sprinkles like kids run wild.

Elves on the counters, they plot and they scheme,
Plotting to turn this into a dream.
Rolling out dough, oh the mess we create,
But laughter and joy are the best kind of fate.

Marshmallow clouds on a cocoa sea,
Our gingerbread army, as brave as can be.
Decorating soldiers, oh what a sight,
With candy canes ready to join in the fight.

In frosted wonderlands, smiles abound,
Each wacky creation spreads joy all around.
As the oven hums softly, our hearts beat as one,
With giggles and sweetness, we've only just begun!

A Dance of Cinnamon and Cloves

Twirl and spin with laughter and spice,
In this merry dance, nothing's precise.
Cinnamon winks from the jar on the shelf,
As we blend in the joy, just being ourselves.

Clove and nutmeg join the fun,
A sprinkle of chaos, and then we run.
Red noses peeking, with frosting to taste,
A chocolate explosion, oh what a haste!

The cookie parade, they march with delight,
Puffed and frosted, they steal the night.
Whiskers of sugar make everyone grin,
Under the laughter, let the fun begin!

In this sweet symphony, all fears take flight,
With giggles and treats, everything's bright.
Culinary jesters make chaos their crown,
In this baking circus, we'll never frown!

Holiday Hearth Harmony

Gathered 'round the hearth, we sing a tune,
With floury hands and a big spoon.
Ginger snaps that laugh, and cookies that cheer,
Every tasty moment brings family near.

The blender rumbles, what a crazy sound,
Like reindeer with hiccups, joy knows no bound.
Sticky fingers dance, a warm, merry glow,
In the chaos we love, our hearts overflow.

Frosting fiascos, we try to create,
Artistic attempts, like a playful debate.
With icing on noses and laughter galore,
In this happy madness, who could want more?

So here's to the cheer, in every single bite,
With humor and joy, our futures are bright.
Through each silly moment, we weave strong ties,
In the warmth of this hearth, true love never lies.

Cheery Confections and Wishes

In a whirlwind of flour, we dance and we play,
Sprinkling laughter in our own special way.
The dough thinks it's funny, it jumps and it rolls,
While cheeks turn to doughnuts and laughter consoles.

With candy canes laughing, we shape and we mold,
Tell tales of the season, as sweetness unfolds.
The oven hums tunes of a jolly old chap,
While giggles erupt from our floury trap.

Twirl of Tinsel and Dough

A pinch of this sparkly, a dash of that too,
As we twirl through the kitchen like elves in a zoo.
Our hats all askew, oh what a strange sight,
With sprinkles like stars, we'll shine through the night.

The clock's ticking loudly, and yet we don't mind,
For gales of pure joy are the best kind of bind.
We sprinkle some giggles, we roll out the cheer,
These moments of madness bring loved ones near.

Whisking Up the Spirit of Giving

With whisks in our hands and smirks on our face,
We craft little goodies, a sweet kind of race.
"Don't eat that one yet!" we shout in delight,
As crumbs turn to treasures, a sugary sight.

A serious game of 'taste it, oh dear!'
Each nibble provoking a chuckle, a cheer.
Like little sugar ninjas, we sneak and we grin,
For presents are best when shared with a spin.

The Sweetness of Togetherness

In our sweet little corner, the laughter erupts,
With frosting like armor, we battle and cup.
The little ones giggle, as sprinkles take flight,
While gingerbread warriors march into the night.

The kitchen is chaotic, a delicious charade,
Where every mishap brings smiles that won't fade.
Together we savor, the joy on our plates,
For moments like these are our holly-day fates.

Frosting Wishes on a Firelit Night

In the kitchen, chaos reigns,
With flour clouds and silly stains.
The spatula dances, a jolly show,
While the taste testers steal the dough.

Laughter bubbles, a sweet delight,
As we smudge frosting left and right.
Cookies shaped like all things absurd,
A reindeer with a very long word!

The timer dings, a frantic rush,
Burnt edges make our families hush.
We salvage what we can with glee,
Crafting treats that are fun to see!

A Pinch of Nutmeg and Nostalgia

The nutmeg jar is tipped and spilled,
Cinnamon sneezes, the air is filled.
Grandma's recipe gets a twist,
Imperfect batches that can't be missed.

Sugar plums dance on plates of cheer,
While cousins argue about who's near.
The ginger forms a curious shape,
A cookie monster with a cape!

We snicker at the mess we made,
A batter slip, a joyful trade.
Whisking dreams into a creamy swirl,
With every laugh, the memories unfurl!

Candy-Cane Charms and Cozy Nights

The candy canes are in a fight,
A battle of who's twirled just right.
Red and white in a sticky heap,
Sweet dreams linger, the flavors seep.

Hot cocoa spills, a frothy grin,
Whipped cream clouds are ready to win.
Marshmallow snowmen stand in rows,
A snowy scene where laughter flows.

Sipping slowly by the brightening fire,
With every sip, our spirits higher.
Wishes made with every clink,
In this cozy night, we hardly think!

A Patchwork of Flavorful Traditions

We gather 'round with rolling pins,
Flour our hair, where the fun begins.
Each cookie a tale of joy and cheer,
Tasting crunchy memories so dear.

A pinch of laughter, a dash of fun,
In our circus kitchen, none can outrun.
Sprinkles fly like little stars,
As we create our culinary memoirs.

The oven hums a merry tune,
Each bursting flavor makes us swoon.
As we nibble on our crispy art,
We know these moments fill the heart!

Homeward Bound with Warm Delights

In a kitchen, laughter stirs,
Flour flies like fuzzy furs.
Mixing giggles, humming tunes,
A sprinkle here brings happy boons.

Silly shapes, a curious crew,
A ginger house with a candy view.
Frosting battles on the floor,
Who knew fun could taste like more?

Warm aromas fill the air,
As we dance without a care.
With every cookie, joy expands,
Crafting sweetness with our hands.

So grab a morsel, have a bite,
These merry treats are pure delight.
With friends around, we twirl and cheer,
Here's to laughter, joy, and cheer!

The Gift of Flavorful Friends

Gather round, the time is nigh,
With sticky fingers and a pie.
We measure fun by the cup,
And watch the pancake syrup sup.

Our friends arrive with bags filled tight,
Baking mats and aprons bright.
The oven's prepped for chaos and cheer,
A sprinkle fight, oh dear, oh dear!

Rolling dough with glee in sight,
Creating chaos, a tasty plight.
Ghosts and stars and silly looks,
The real magic's in our cooks.

When all is done, we sit and snack,
With cookies piled up, there's no lack.
Laughter lingers in every taste,
With sugary joy, we dance with haste.

Winter's Treats of Delight

A snowy day, a tasty quest,
We whip and swirl, we're at our best.
Wiggly dough, it flops and rolls,
Who knew sugar had such goals?

The kitchen's filled with clinks and clangs,
As spatulas dance and laughter hangs.
Dip in chocolate, a gooey mess,
More sugar sprinkles? Yes, yes, yes!

Ginger folk with gumdrop acts,
Telling tales in crunchy packs.
The frosting spills like winter sleighs,
Making messes in the funniest ways.

In every bite a cheer we find,
With sweetened friends, we're all aligned.
A taste of joy, a laugh or two,
These treats bring warmth, it's all true!

Cheery Carols and Sugar Crystals

With every scoop, a song we sing,
Mixing tunes with flour brings.
Eggs and spice in jubilant flings,
The joy of baking is our king.

The silly shapes dance on the tray,
Gummy bears sing, hip-hip hooray!
Frosted joy spreads wide and far,
Candy sprinkles shining like stars.

As friends arrive, the laughter grows,
With cookie monsters hiding in rows.
Underneath the tinsel bright,
We nibble treats through the snowy night.

The carols echo, laughter loud,
In this joy, we're all so proud.
Desserts uniting, sugar divine,
With every bite, we intertwine.

Sweet Houses of Whimsy

In a kitchen where chaos reigns,
Ginger dough flies like runaway trains.
With sprinkles raining from the sky,
Even the cat has given a try.

Rolling pins wage a battle loud,
Flour clouds gather like a fluffy shroud.
Cookie cutters, a quirky crew,
Fear not, my friend, we'll make it through!

Frosting fights turn laughter to song,
Debating if candy can possibly belong.
A door adorned with a gumdrop ring,
Every bite's a hilarious little fling.

At the table, moments get sticky,
Sweet creations can turn quite tricky.
We toast with cookies, and all is right,
In this whimsical world, we delight!

The Spice of Togetherness

Measurements are lost in laughter's game,
Sugar spills like the wildest flame.
Spoons collide in an epic mix,
Flavors blend with a few crazy tricks.

An apron is worn like a regal crown,
With frosting smeared from head to gown.
The oven hums a jolly tune,
While dough takes shape under a watchful moon.

Mischief lurks in every corner,
As ginger warriors become a foreigner.
Candy canes march in a sweet parade,
The merry mayhem of our lovely charade.

Amidst sugar sprinkles and giggles galore,
We craft our memories forevermore.
In the warmth of this playful mess,
The joy of it all, we truly confess!

Frosted Dreams in Flour

In a swirl of sugar, I find my glee,
Sifting flour like a snowflake spree.
Gumdrop eyes stare with delight,
As we decorate through the merry night.

Laughter bubbles in a bowl of cream,
Mixing moments like a silly dream.
A cheeky grin as we taste the dough,
Who knew sweet treats could steal the show?

Licorice strings dance in the air,
Chocolate chips, they're everywhere!
Gingerbread folks laugh and prance,
In this sticky, sweet, silly romance.

With spatulas raised, we make a toast,
To floury fun we cherish the most.
In this kitchen, joy takes a stance,
In icing and giggles, we find our chance!

A Symphony of Sugar and Spice

A merry cacophony fills the room,
As flour spills out like a fluffy bloom.
Spices join in a lively dance,
While cookie shapes take a goofy stance.

Laughter rings as the timer beeps,
A sprinkle fight awakens from sleeps.
With chocolate rivers and peppermint dreams,
Every bite evokes victorious screams.

A castle of cookies, grand and tall,
Pillars made of candies, we built them all.
Gingerbread laughter spills from the seams,
In a world where whimsy reigns like streams.

With each crunchy bite, we share delight,
In sugary bliss, everything feels right.
With every giggle, our hearts entwine,
In this festive joy, all things align!

The Magic of Molasses Moments

In a bowl, the syrup swirls,
Flour flies like magic pearls.
Spices dance in jolly cheer,
Watch out, flour! The dough is here!

Sugar men in hats so tall,
Should I make them short or small?
Laughter echoes, kids in glee,
Whisking up a calamity!

Rolling out the sticky stuff,
Shaped like reindeer, oh so tough!
A bite and giggle, what a sight,
A cookie war breaks out tonight!

In the oven, they start to whine,
"Don't forget us! We're divine!"
When the timer dings, hooray!
Let's eat them all without delay!

Tinsel and Dough: A Festive Mix

Tinsel twirls on the kitchen shelf,
While I wrestle with myself.
The dough won't stick, it wants to slide,
My apron's now a doughnut ride!

Sprinkles scatter like confetti,
The cat thinks it's a game, how petty!
I laugh as frosting lands on my nose,
Oops! Who knew sugar could pose?

Baking sheets become my stage,
Each cookie a bright, sugary page.
My ginger crew, let's make a dance,
With each bite, comes a giggle-glance!

The clock strikes, the cookies blaze,
What a sight! They're in a craze!
Take a bite and what a fight,
Half for me and half for fright!

Ginger-Scented Smiles

In a whirl of spice and laughter,
The kitchen hums with sweet disaster.
Ginger snaps and giggles play,
Who knew cookies could betray?

Rolling pins are flying high,
One hits me—oh my oh my!
Dough is flopping, what a scene,
How did I make that dough so mean?

Frosting rivers, rainbow streams,
A sugar rush fuels our dreams.
Decorate with crazy flair,
A candy nose, a gummy hair!

The taste test, oh what a mime,
"No, I swear I'm not out of time!"
All's well when laughter's in the air,
And ginger smiles are everywhere!

The Art of Sweetened Generosity

A splash of this, a pinch of cheer,
In a world where cookies steer.
Sharing dough is quite the feat,
When everyone wants the biggest treat!

Little hands all sticky brown,
"I made a bear! It's a clown!"
Frosting on the nose, oh dear,
Is it a snack or a holiday smear?

The mixing bowl's a splendid mess,
Shaping joy is quite the stress.
But when they share their sugary art,
A muffin tin becomes a heart!

At the end, we munch and grin,
Who knew this chaos could win?
With giggles loud and voices bright,
Sweetened love is pure delight!

Echoes of Laughter

In the kitchen, dough took flight,
A flour cloud, what a sight!
Giggling kids, rolling pins swing,
In this chaos, joy can sing.

The dog licks up what we drop,
While we mix, we just can't stop.
Ginger men with crooked smiles,
Dance around, oh what styles!

Savory Treats

A spicy scent fills up the air,
With sneaky bites, we do declare.
Cookies shaped like dogs and cats,
Oven timers? A thing for brats!

Mischief baked in every round,
Nibbled sweets are always found.
Laughter echoes, trust the mix,
Frosting fights bring silly tricks!

Unity in Every Glaze

Sticky fingers, oh what fun,
Together we strategize, run!
With icing bags and sprinkles near,
Creating madness, never fear!

Lumpy frosting on my shoe,
Whipped cream fights? We start anew.
Giggles burst, a joyful scene,
In this mess, we reign supreme!

The Festive Feast of Flavors

Chestnut browns and sugar whites,
Whisking cream until it bites.
An army of sweets lined in rows,
Keeping secrets, nobody knows!

Christmas tunes played on repeat,
As we gather 'round to eat.
Lost a cookie? Not a chance!
In this mayhem, we all dance!

Sugar-coated Memories

Each flavor tells a tale or two,
Of sticky hands and laughter, too.
A bite of spice, a dash of fun,
Every moment shines like sun!

Reminiscing with a smile,
Silly stories last awhile.
Crumbling laughter, sweet delight,
In each bite, our hearts take flight!

Scented Memories in the Air

A whisk went flying, oh dear me,
Flour is dancing, wild and free.
The spatula fell, it made a crash,
Sticky fingers, what a splash!

Oven's a monster, roaring loud,
But the cookies still make us proud.
With sugar sprinkles, we declare,
Joy is baked in every layer.

Ginger men giggle, on the rack,
"Don't eat us now, we'll be a snack!"
Smiles and laughter, we all share,
As scent of spice fills up the air.

So let's get messy, flour in hair,
With these sweet treats, nothing can compare!
From kitchen chaos, fun we'll find,
Scented memories, one of a kind.

Ginger Man and Winter Wishes

A little ginger man with a plan,
He's dancing 'round like a sprightly fan.
"Catch me if you can, but be aware,
I'm faster than the ginger in my hair!"

With frosting smiles that twinkle bright,
He plays all day and into the night.
"Wish upon a cookie, that's my goal,
For warm hearts, laughter, that's my role!"

The snowflakes swirl, casting a spell,
While winter whispers, "All is well."
With every bite, the joy expands,
In a world where gingerbread stands.

So grab your pals, let's sing and cheer,
For the ginger guy brings festive cheer!
In every crinkle and every grin,
We find the magic of joy within.

A Recipe for Warmth

Gather 'round, it's time to mix,
A sprinkle here, a dash of tricks.
First, add laughter, nice and bright,
Followed by hugs, to the right.

A pinch of whims, a dash of glee,
And don't forget the giggling spree!
Stir it well with a smile or two,
This is how we bake our brew.

Shape them as reindeer, or toss a star,
Ginger delights that'll travel far.
Then watch them rise, oh what a sight,
Warmth fills the kitchen, pure delight!

When you take a bite, be ready to grin,
For every nibble, the joy kicks in.
In this recipe, the secret's true,
Love is the ingredient, especially for you!

Cups of Cocoa and Ginger Delight

Grab a cup, cozy and warm,
Cocoa swirls in a chocolaty charm.
With ginger bits and marshmallow fluff,
A perfect potion when times get tough.

Sipping slow while socks are bright,
Candle flames flicker, a dancing light.
We chuckle and spill, but who really cares?
Happiness lives in the messy affairs!

Cinnamon whispers, "Please take a taste!"
With gingerbread bits, we won't let them waste.
The chilly air can't steal our cheer,
For mugs are raised in holiday gear!

So let's toast to joy, with every swig,
As laughter and sweets make our hearts dig.
Cups of cocoa, friends and fun,
In this festive game, we've all just won!

Stars and Sprinkles: A Festive Canvas

In a bowl, flour's a snowy dream,
Sugar's dance with the butter's gleam,
Eggs crack like jokes upon the floor,
As we find giggles we can't ignore.

Rolling dough like a crazy wheel,
Shapes appear, oh what a deal!
Stars and hearts, with shapes galore,
Mom's hat gets dusted, we all roar!

The oven hums like a happy tune,
Silly faces made with a spoon,
Watch those cookie shapes take their flight,
Puffy treasures emerge from the night.

Sprinkles rain like confetti bright,
Making our treats a pure delight,
A laughter-filled kitchen, all aglow,
Creating sweetness, stealing the show.

Whirls of Laughter in the Kitchen

Whisk it fast, let the giggles flow,
Eggs do a dance, just watch them go,
Flour clouds like a snowy boom,
We wear aprons like a funny costume.

Spatulas spin like wands of cheer,
Chocolate chips disappear, oh dear!
Sticky fingers and powdered noses,
Our kitchen chaos, everybody knows this.

The timer dings, we gasp in delight,
Cookies near done, oh, what a sight!
Molded reindeer start to jumble,
Mom's new recipe ends in a tumble.

As we taste test, giggles erupt,
Laughter and crumbs—we're all corrupt,
Each slice we share brings more than glee,
In this swirling mess, we find our spree.

Sweet Scents of Yuletide Bliss

Mixing and stirring with carefree flair,
Sugar sprinkles fly through the air,
Baking sheets like canvases wait,
For chocolate to swirly-fy our fate.

Whiffs of ginger tease our noses,
Laughter spills out, just like roses,
Muffins wobble and cookies grin,
A floured dusting covers our chin.

In the oven, magic starts to grow,
Puffing treats all in a row,
Oven mitts dance, they do a jig,
As we snicker at the marshmallow big.

Tasting each batch brings squeals and cheers,
Joyful moments from front to rears,
In the delight of what we create,
We've made a mess, but it's truly great!

The Joy of Sharing a Slice

Gather 'round for a slice of cheer,
Cake-shaped wonders, oh my dear!
Frostings swirl in a colorful spree,
Each bite a giggle, you're sure to agree.

Cake shaky legs that wobble with grace,
If it tips over, we'll laugh in its face,
Sprinkled with stories, each slice we share,
In this own little world, there's fun everywhere.

With every giggle, the cake gets tall,
Silly toppers, we'll stack one and all,
A bite of laughter tastes just so sweet,
In this kitchen, joy is our treat.

As we share our slices and tales galore,
Life feels like one big bakery store,
With crumbs on our faces and smiles so wide,
Every moment is a magical ride.

The Warmth of Cinnamon Wishes

Whisking dreams in a bowl of cheer,
A pinch of chaos stirs, never fear!
Cinnamon whispers with a naughty grin,
Let the holiday mishaps begin!

Frosting battles on the counter's stage,
The gingerbread men have taken the cage.
Do they know that they might end up eaten?
A sweet little joke, the giggles are beaten.

Rolling dough becomes a dance routine,
With flour on noses, we look quite obscene.
The mixer's on strike, it's starting to hum,
Is it just me or is that cinnamon fun?

The scent fills the air, with sprinkles aplenty,
Who knew yummies could be quite so silly?
As we gather round to share a bite,
Warmth spreads in giggles, a purest delight!

Cookies and Cheer in Every Bite

In a kitchen filled with flour dust,
Ginger men are squawking, oh what a fuss!
Heads rolling on the counter, oh dear,
Do you think they'll run away in fear?

Sprinkles scatter like confetti in air,
Each cookie is a treasure, handle with care.
One sneezed into the mix, oh how it laughed,
Now we have cookies that smell like a draft!

Frosting faces in a wild array,
Who made the biggest mess? We all want to play.
Giggles echo, and the oven beeps,
We dance with joy while the batter sleeps.

When the timer dings like a chubby bell,
Out pops the laughter, can you just smell?
Each bite brings giggles, with smiles so bright,
Cookies of cheer, oh what a delight!

Crumbs of Love and Laughter

A chaotic kitchen, what a sight to see,
Gingerbread creatures playing hide-and-seek.
Flour footprints lead to mischievous plots,
They may be sweet, but trust me, they're hot!

Chocolate chips talk back with smirks,
Dough's like a dance, oh, how it lurks.
A spatula sword in a frosting fight,
Victory tastes like a sugary bite!

Oh crumbs fly like confetti, what a thrill,
With laughter and joy, we couldn't sit still.
"Who's got the icing?" someone does cheer,
While we all giggle, it's time to smear!

Gathered together, sharing our cheer,
Each crumb tells a story we hold so dear.
The taste of fun, memories ignite,
In every sweet moment, life feels just right!

Sugar-Plum Visions and Holiday Delights

A wild concoction in a bowl so wide,
Sugar plums giggle as they start to slide.
Sprinkling hopes like fairy dust,
This joyful chaos is a must!

Sapling-sized cookies dance on the table,
While the gingerbread man looks quite unstable.
"Let me stand!" he shouts with a stomp,
Too many sweets, he's ready to plump!

Muffin tops wiggle in a jolly parade,
'Caution!' we shout, or it might just invade.
Each bite brings joy, laughter's delight,
In this funny kitchen, everything's right!

The oven hums a sweet melody,
As we decorate dreams in pure harmony.
With visions of sugar, we dance in the light,
Celebrating together, oh what a night!

Cozy Kitchen Chronicles

In the kitchen where flour flies,
Sprinkling sugar, oh what a surprise!
Ginger snaps dance on the floor,
As we battle cookies, what a uproar!

Rolling pins are our trusty swords,
While we chant our festive chords.
I dropped a spoon, it made a sound,
Laughter erupts, joy all around!

A little frosting, a dash of cheer,
The doughnut hole's now a reindeer!
Batter's on my nose, what a sight,
What a messy, merry night!

In the end, we taste our plight,
Gingerbread men in a goofy fight.
Every cookie has its charm,
In this kitchen, we cause no harm!

A Canvas of Sugar and Joy

With a whisk in hand, we make a splash,
Frosting everywhere, oh what a crash!
Cookies shaped like stars and moons,
Glittering sprinkles like festive balloons!

Our dough's a monster, soft and warm,
It wiggles and jiggles, causing alarm.
We build a house, it leans to the right,
Watch out, gingerbread, you might take flight!

Chocolate chips rain like tiny pearls,
As laughter and fun create whirlpools.
Piping bags explode with a pop,
Decorations tumble, but we won't stop!

At the table, we dine with glee,
A feast of cookies, just you and me.
With every bite, a giggle is passed,
In our sugary world, happiness lasts!

Sprinkled Happiness

Sprinkles cascade like colorful rain,
If I wear them, am I insane?
Rolling dough looks like a bear's hug,
Who knew baking could be so snug?

The oven giggles with a warm purr,
As I dance around, hear me stir!
Flour fights and sugar bliss,
What a hilarious baking twist!

Ginger men wear hats made of cream,
Every bite feels like a dream.
A cookie army ready to charge,
In this sugar war, we'll be at large!

With each bite, joy melts on the tongue,
Singing carols, we're all so young.
A sprinkle explosion, what a delight,
In our sweet chaos, all feels right!

Threads of Tradition

Grandma's recipe, a treasure we find,
With each secret step, we unwind.
She says, 'Just a pinch, don't go wild!'
But here comes the chaos, we're laughing like a child!

Cinnamon dances with ginger's twirl,
Cookies tumble and watch them swirl.
A frosting fight breaks out, oh dear!
Who knew such fun could come from here?

The aroma wafts like a warm embrace,
In our frosted, sweet little space.
Each cookie tells a story so bright,
Merry traditions, oh what a sight!

As we gather 'round with treats galore,
Sharing joy, we always want more.
With laughter echoing through the night,
These merry moments feel so right!

Gingerbread Houses Under Twinkling Stars

In a kitchen where flour flies,
And dough starts to dance and rise,
Sugar rush, sprinkles on the floor,
Who knew dessert could mean a war?

Chortles echo, laughter loud,
A marshmallow crowned gingerbread crowd,
Edible homes and jellybean lands,
Each piece built by creative hands.

Candy canes form a sweet defense,
Against cookie thieves, it makes no sense,
Frosting rivers and gumdrop trees,
We never thought baking could bring such glee!

Under the stars, our confections glow,
A gingerbread kingdom, oh what a show!
With giggles and crumbs scattered wide,
This festive fun can't be denied!

The Joy of Mixing Tradition

Butter, sugar, oh what a delight,
Whisk it fast, we'll have a bite,
Eggs leaping in with joy and cheer,
Who knew mixing could bring such beer?

The clan gathers, chaos unfolds,
Grandma's secrets, too funny to hold,
Spices sprinkled like silly jokes,
We're baking treats, not just for folks!

Cinnamon whispers, nutmeg shouts,
As flour clouds swirl, laughter sprout,
Traditions twisted, oh so absurd,
The kitchen's now a laughter bird.

When the oven bell begins its ring,
We dance around while cookies sing,
Embracing fun, forget the strife,
In sticky mess, we find our life!

Seasonal Smiles in Every Bite

A cookie ninja with icing skills,
Sculpting treats while ignoring spills,
In every bite, a giggle hides,
Sugar secrets, joy abides.

Sprinkle fights and doughy traps,
Flour hats and doughy naps,
Taste testers with eyes so wide,
Sweet tooth warriors, side by side.

Each bite crunches, joy unleashed,
Smiles abound, happiness increased,
A world of sweetness, none can fight,
Seasonal magic wrapped up tight.

With each nibble, laughter grows,
The sweetest battle, everyone knows,
We're all winners, what a sight,
In every bite, pure delight!

Enchanted Dough and Icing Wishes

The dough rolls out like magic dreams,
Caught in the shimmer of icing beams,
With every swirl and twirl we make,
Noticing how our sides do ache.

Magical sprinkles scatter about,
Joyful shouts, "Oh, let's see who shouts!"
As shapes emerge from our merry game,
It's clear that none of us are the same.

The oven giggles and the spatula sings,
Mixing giggles with powdered flings,
Each creation gets its own special name,
These tasty treasures, oh what a claim!

With icing wishes shaped with flair,
We build our dreams beyond compare,
In laughter, love, and sugary bliss,
We seal our joy with a doughy kiss!

The Aroma of Festive Cheer

In the kitchen, a swirl of delight,
Flour flies in a chaotic flight.
Sugar dances on the countertop,
With giggles that never seem to stop.

Whisking eggs with a comical flair,
Batter splatters everywhere!
A dash of cinnamon, a pinch of whim,
Each calamity makes the laughter brim.

Ovens roaring like a festive choir,
Cookies bubble, a sugary fire.
The clock ticks down with a mischievous grin,
Who knew chaos could taste so akin?

With sprinkles thrown like confetti gold,
A whimsical story of sweetness bold.
Let's toast to the mess, to the fun we've grown,
In this delightful chaos, we've found our home.

Cookies that Share a Secret

Gather 'round, all the treats will speak,
In laughter's embrace, we dare to peek.
Each cookie winks from its frosted plate,
Whispering tales of the sugary fate.

Jolly shapes in red and green,
Chubby reindeer, a cookie queen.
They plot mischief with every bite,
In this sugary world, everything's right.

Peeking from tins with a cheeky grin,
These delicious spies invite you in.
"Take a nibble, discover our lore,
Each crumb, a secret, a taste to adore!"

With giggles that bubble and spirits that soar,
Each bite contains laughter and so much more.
Join the feast, let the merriment flow,
For these charming cookies put on quite the show!

Flour Dust and Merry Laughter

Flour dust rises like a snowstorm bright,
Laughter erupts, what a glorious sight!
Rolling pins flying through the air,
With happy hearts, we're beyond compare.

Buttercream battles and frosting fights,
Giggling chefs in their cocoa tights.
The floor is a canvas of sweet delight,
As we craft our treats from daylight to night.

Sprinkling joy with a playful hand,
In this oven of warmth, we take a stand.
Flavors collide like a festive parade,
With joy overflowing, we're never afraid.

Each creation is joy, each mishap a song,
In this bustling joy, we feel we belong.
With aprons askew, we watch our treats rise,
In the fluff of our laughter, the magic belies.

A Kingdom of Sugar and Spice

Welcome to our kingdom, a sugary gleam,
Where candy castles fulfill every dream.
Marzipan bridges and licorice lanes,
Joyful giggles amidst sugar rains.

Gummy bears march, the jelly is bright,
These tasty soldiers, oh what a sight!
Crafting a kingdom where flavors play,
Building our empire in the sweet ballet.

Chocolate rivers run through cookie trees,
Whimsical wonders put our minds at ease.
Each sprinkle of joy, a spark of delight,
In our land of sweets, everything feels right.

With every nibble, our laughter will grow,
In this kingdom of sugar, love's sweetest show.
Let's revel together, in sugar and cheer,
In our festively bright frontier!

Heartwarming Treats for All

In the kitchen, flour flies,
As giggles mix with spice.
A doughy blob starts to rise,
A craft, oh what a dice!

Rolling pins take flight,
Like wands in a wizard's hand.
Cookies dance under the light,
A crunchy, sugary band.

Shapes of stars and jolly men,
With icing smiles that gleam.
Could we eat them all again?
Our laughter is the cream!

Oh, the smells that fill the air,
Like magic in a bowl.
Each bite, a cheerful flair,
A warm and happy soul.

Lovingly Layered Treasures

There's a cake that's stacked so high,
It might just touch the sky.
With layers green and sprinkles spry,
We'll eat it, oh my my!

The frosting flops and slides away,
A sticky, sweet ballet.
Oops! One fell to the bouquet,
The cat leaps in, hooray!

Whisking eggs with delight,
The kitchen looks like a storm.
We savor each silly bite,
As laughter keeps us warm.

With every forkful we share,
We giggle and we cheer.
Messy fun without a care,
It's the best time of year!

Savoring the Season of Goodwill

A scoop of joy in every scoop,
With friends who sing and swoop.
In a merry, bustling troupe,
We toss dough like a loop!

The oven's like a cozy hug,
As we dance on flour dust.
Smells of nutmeg give a tug,
In merry, blissful trust.

Sipping drinks all warm and bright,
We toast to cheer and fun.
Drifting in the snowy night,
Our hearts unite as one.

So rise, ye treats, all snug and round,
Let laughter fill the space.
With every joy, we will be found,
Together in this place.

Sweet Whispers Inviting Cold Nights

As winter whispers soft and low,
We curl up with cookies, oh!
The chilly winds make us glow,
With ginger hugs, we flow.

Piping bags filled to the brim,
Creating art with every whim.
A sprinkle here, a frosting trim,
Our joy is never dim!

The timer dings with cheerful cheer,
The world outside is white.
In this cozy, joyful sphere,
We celebrate the night.

Mirth and flavors intertwine,
With smiles set afire.
In this magic, love divine,
We all sit round, inspired!

A Celebration in Every Batch

In the kitchen, sprinkles fly,
Flour dancing, oh my my!
Chocolate chips hide, what a plot,
Taste testers love them, give it a shot!

Rolling dough like a big, fat cat,
With a pinch of this and a dash of that.
Ginger men frolic, how they prance,
But who's the one who spilled the chance?

Iced with laughter, it's quite a sight,
Candy canes gleaming, oh what a bite!
Sugar and spice, do we even care?
Just one more cookie? Well, maybe a pair!

So grab your friends for a cookie war,
In this sweet chaos, we always want more.
Giggles and crumbs, a blast we spin,
With every batch, feel the joy within!

Morsels of Merriment

A sprinkle here, a sprinkle there,
They called it cooking, but it's more like care!
The oven's hot, don't burn the batch,
Who knew flour could cause such a scratch?

An army of smiles in the cookie tray,
A bite of madness in every play.
Gingersnaps waltzing, what a sight,
With frosting shoes, they feel so right!

Taste-testing fails, another one bites,
But who's counting in these snickering nights?
Caramel drizzle, too sticky to fight,
Oh, let's add more; it'll be all right!

So gather round for a laughter spree,
With every chomp, we let out a squeak.
In this cheerful mess, let's spread the cheer,
In morsels of joy that bring us near!

The Cheery Confectioner's Tale

Once a baker with a twinkling eye,
Whipped up something that made birds fly!
Ginger folks dancing across the floor,
Error or magic? Who keeps the score?

Rolling pins ready, it's time for fun,
With a dash of mishaps that weigh a ton.
Frosted laughter on the kitchen walls,
Waiting for sweets, oh, how the joy calls!

The whisk has secrets it's learning to tell,
Mixing the giggles, oh how they swell.
Choco-mistakes, an icing parade,
Creating the sweets that we can't evade!

So cheers to the mess, the joyful hearts,
In every confection, a life that starts.
From spatulas winks to a sugary scoff,
In the tale of a baker, we can't get enough!

Frosty Toppings and Laughter Lines

In a whirl of frosting, smiles collide,
With each cookie made, we take a ride.
Marshmallows tumble, oh what a scene,
Gathering giggles, where we've all been!

Cookies like snowflakes, all with their flair,
Some look perfect, others in despair.
Yelling 'Wait, look! That one can dance!'
While we munch on treats, we give them a chance!

Frosty toppings that wiggle with glee,
Every sweet bite feels like jubilee.
The dough has stories, it's twirling around,
In the laughter lines, joy will abound!

So raise a spatula, let's make a toast,
For every sweet moment, we love the most.
With bitterness banished, we savor the rhyme,
In the kitchen of fun, we're freezing time!

Magic in Every Rolling Pin

With a pinch of spice and a twirl so grand,
The rolling pin dances, it's got a plan.
Flour flies high, like snow in the air,
Watch out, my friend, it might end in a flare!

The dough starts to giggle, what a sight to behold,
As we shape little figures, all shiny and bold.
But one little man slipped, oh what a fall,
Now he's stuck to the counter, what a call!

With icing emergencies and sprinkles galore,
We laugh 'till we cry as we sweep off the floor.
These sweet little mishaps bring joy in a rush,
A cookie catastrophe turns into a crush!

So grab your best spatula, hold onto your hat,
This kitchen's a circus, and we love it like that!
Dough flying, kids laughing, all merry and bright,
We'll feast on these blunders, oh what a delight!

A Symphony of Sweetness

In the kitchen we gather, the band's all around,
With spoons as our batons, we create quite a sound.
The mixer goes whirr, like a tune from a show,
And the cookies start dancing, don't, you know?

The sugar sings high, the butter hums low,
As cinnamon swirls make our melodies flow.
A second of silence, then pop! – a surprise,
The dough's in the oven, it's rising with sighs!

Now the scents fill the room, a warm blanket of cheer,
As we gather our friends, and hold each one dear.
But one cookie rebel, with chocolate chips brave,
Decided to run, oh, how we all gave!

So let's toast with our mugs, full of cocoa divine,
Next round's on the chef, who can't keep from the line.
This symphony's sweet, just a tad out of key,
But it's filled with love, and that's harmony!

Cheer from the Sugar Bowl

In the cupboard, a treasure, a sugar white mound,
With a scoop from the bowl, we make joy abound.
Sprinkles fly like confetti, oh what a blast,
But one snooty ginger tried to make it last!

He claimed he was perfect, a cookie elite,
While the others just giggled, admitting defeat.
'Cause who needs a crown when you're all full of fun?
A sprinkle parade, we all know who's won!

The icing's a canvas, let the fun begin,
With faces and stories, we can't help but grin.
But Mr. Ginger missed the joke of the day,
When his bow tie fell off – what a baking bouquet!

So let's cheer for the sugar, the spice on our trays,
For laughter and love in so many ways.
With each whisk and giggle, let's raise up a cheer,
For joy served on plates – it's the best time of year!

Kitchen Chronicles of Yuletide

With aprons as capes, we are heroes today,
The kitchen our kingdom, in our own special way.
Flour on our noses, like badges of flair,
We're ready for mischief, let's tempt a dessert scare!

Our spatulas clash, like swords in delight,
While hitters of these batter fights bring a sweet plight.
The oven's a warm hug, but watch out! – beware,
A cookie brigade could spin through the air!

With laughter and chaos, the stories unfold,
Of failed soufflés, and dough that won't hold.
Yet through all the stumbles, we cherish each treat,
For memories are made with each sweet mess we beat!

So gather your friends, let's fill up the scene,
With frosting and giggles, we'll keep our hearts keen.
These chronicles show, it's the funny and fun
That make this time special, for everyone!

A Tale of Spices and Spirits

In a kitchen, flour flies free,
Ginger leaps like a bouncy bee.
Nuts hide under the rolling pin,
Awaiting their time to bring the grin.

Cinnamon winks from the spice rack,
Nutmeg's plotting a sneaky attack.
Sugar trolls dance on the rogue heat,
They tickle our noses with smells so sweet.

With each cookie, a giggle erupts,
As doughy monsters say, "We're all cupped!"
The oven hums a merry tune,
While ginger folks plot their afternoon.

So raise a whisk for a toast to this,
To sprightly spices and sugary bliss.
Laughter and crumbs fill the air,
In this merry land of culinary dare.

Nutty Narratives Under the Mistletoe

Under twinkling lights we assemble,
With tales of nuts that wiggle and tremble.
Almonds whisper, 'We're quite dapper!'
While walnuts nod and giggle in clapper.

The cocoa's brewing quite a plot,
As marshmallows dance and take a shot.
Cherries chuckle, ripe for some cheer,
Their sticky antics bring forth a sneer.

Flour swims like a snowstorm bright,
Powdering noses, what a sight!
With each sprinkle, our spirits soar,
The oven's done, now let's explore!

Gather round for tales so grand,
Of nutty adventures so sweet and bland.
We'll feast and laugh well into the night,
With treats so silly, and each bite just right.

The Floury Footprints of Family

In a swirl of dough, we take our stand,
With floury footprints across the land.
Grandma's giggles, a sprinkle of sass,
While kids dive in with an 'oops' and a clash.

Raisins roll like little spies,
Peeking out with their wrinkled eyes.
Silly faces of frosted delight,
As cookie soldiers prepare for a fight.

Doughy disasters cause everyone to laugh,
With sprinkles scattered like a playful staff.
The whisk takes flight, an aerial show,
As we whip up joy in a flurry of dough!

Shaped like trees, or stars oh so bright,
Each cookie a tale, a sweet little sight.
In this bond of flour and sweetest fun,
We cherish each moment, till the day is done.

Enchanted Tables and Sweetened Tales

At a table adorned in a sugary bliss,
The laughter and crumbs form a family kiss.
With chocolate drizzles that spill like dreams,
Each bite brings giggles and silly schemes.

Stars shine bright over plates piled high,
While sticky fingers wave 'hello' to the sky.
The jolly old fellow shares stories so bold,
Of gingerbread armies and treasures of gold.

Frosted fun leads our taste buds on,
With berry grins from the break of dawn.
Bite-sized bites whisper charms so dear,
While the mismatched crew sheds every fear.

So gather around, bring your quirks and cheer,
To the table where joy is the sweetest here.
In enchanted whispers, our laughter will flow,
As sweetened tales dance in the warm, sparkling glow.

Milton Keynes UK
Ingram Content Group UK Ltd.
UKHW020045271124
451585UK00012B/1069